Hunter-Gatherer

Hunter-Gatherer

R.T. Smith

Livingston Press
The University of West Alabama

ISBN 0-942979-34-6, paperback
ISBN 0-942979-33-8, cloth

Library of Congress Cataloguing in Publication # 96-76094

Manufactured in the United States of America.

Text layout and design by Joe Taylor
Manuscript typing and proofreading by Melissa Boand, Beth Grant, Lee
Holland-Moore, and Tina Naremore
Cover photo by Amanda Stuart

Printed by Birmingham Publishing

Grateful acknowledgement to the following:
Carolina Quarterly: Alter All; *Charlotte Poetry Review:* A Catholic Education;
Cimarron Review: Mist Net, Painting Osceola; *Crucible:* Apple Voyage, In Harvest
Season, Lithograph, Watercolorist; *Free Lunch:* Kilcoolie Fern; *Gaia:* Chore; *Georgia
Review:* Hunter-Gatherer; *International Poetry Review:* Playing the Bones; *James
Dickey Newsletter:* Haft Blossom; *The Journal:* Drift; *Keltic Fringe:* On Laraine's
Grave Hill; *Lullwater Review:* Walter Anderson in Mississippi; *New Collage:*
Nachtmusik; *New Virginia Review:* Chickadees; *North Dakota Review:* Birds, In the
Vigor of Memory; *Pembroke Magazine:* Crockett in the Mountains; *Poem:* Audubon's
Cardinal; *Poet & Critic:* Life List, Sabbath in Donegal, The Uses of Enchantment;
Southern Humanities Review: A Brady Photograph of Lee; *Southern Poetry Review:*
Ghost Dance, Legacy, Shrine, Walter Anderson's J; *Sycamore Review:* Fire Blight;
Tamaqua: Goyathlay; *Texas Review:* Grandfather's Hearth; *Yarrow:* Tinkers, Water
Moth.

"Goyathlay" was included in MacMillan's *Literature: A Contemporary Introduction.*

"The Names of Trees," "Legacy," and "Haft Blossom" were included in a chapbook
entitled *The Names of Trees,* from Night Shade Press.

LIVINGSTON PRESS
STATION 22
THE UNIVERSITY OF WEST ALABAMA
LIVINGSTON, AL 35470

TABLE OF CONTENTS

Other books by the Author:

The Hollow Log Lounge
From The High Dive
The Cardinal Heart
Faith (short stories)
*Trespasse*r

for Scott Ward

1.

HUNTER-GATHERER

for A.R. Ammons

The way the magpie scavenges
string, leaf-dregs, twigs & bits
of stray glitter to weave & cantilever

his nest—that cliché says one
way it is. In a winter copse of
fishbone hardwoods arrowing up &

the rare spruce or longleaf evergreen,
I am all eyes till some sliver
of image rhymes with the half-dark

in me. Then I am the tripped
snare or quick fingers greedy for
chestnut or sarvisberry, a cupric blue

streak of evening sky hammered
into swampwater. I can
sniff the badger scat or kneel

for the cleft heart of a buck's
hoofprint in scumbled mud. I can
backtrack & read the scatter of shocked

grackles over the larches to guess
where provender runs or lies still
with its secret. The art of

stalking in a dry time is mine, as well as
blending with the stealth of hickory
bark in the autumn fog. Listening

for the wind I can circle disturbed
dirt with my idiom & gumption. What I
have is the diction & cracked syntax

to glimpse & gather. By contour
& leaf-twirl I drift with a purpose
over hedge & ha-ha where the gestures

of the tracked grasses & scree
in the creekbed offer conjugation,
declension, the slow growth of meaning.

Cast-off antler & bullsnake slough,
hornet helmet of gray, the whip-o-will's
starlight chirr—these syllables are my

appetite—possum pie, trout meat, doe
steak & dove, persimmon & crabapple, wild
savor of the ground squirrel's thigh. This

is what I'm hunting with so many names
under jay-rasp & southerly gusts
shaving the edge off vision. I will

follow water's low roll & rush
to taste & touch the structure
of what was & wants to be. I make it up

but shape it from mica chips
& milk fog on the calm water,
dirty weather of all sorts,

spring storm, July miasma or mere
shower. In draw, on rimrock,
on my belly in the meadow, I am after

skim ice & stumprot, bitteroot & dogwood
stars, quail roost, ramp
& volunteer plum, the snort & tusk-scrape

of a feral pig pissed off at frost. One
hedgehog quill in the canebrake
can bewilder me. If

a hangdog widow-maker bough snarled
in high vines wants me, here I am,
bending for pine seeds that sleep

under path-trample & dream of the wildfire
that will rouse them & fill
their new limbs with birds' razzle-dazzle. Here

a leg hinge & ligament of a lost
dog, there a salt lick & lizard
skitter, shoal snag & lichen shine.

I fetch them & fabricate, but
this is not to say I venerate
the primitive only. Toad spittle

& cherokee rose, hawk circle & the crow—
shadow's caw are just my guides. Birdpoint
& slingstone, lead pellets, any

missile to stun a rabbit launching
for gorse cover or hutch: I have my
methods of collecting even the blue

moon that proves itself over
the gnarled locusts just seven
times in nineteen years. On a backbone

ridge I may study the wren yolk & bacon
streak of dawn or stand in skunk-wonder,
hoping for cleansing rain. Jay spiel

& buzzard spiral, nettle & pod, hornbeam,
popple, bayou bisque & the deerfly's
homily all haunt me, lure my mind & its

receding horizon through hawkweed,
trillium, rushes whitewashed with heron
lime. What logos, tropos & topos in this

biosphere serve me? This is the way I slide &
baffle, evade the coffin satin
of the cottonmouth's yawn & massagua's

alarm, attend to the rattlebone
& smolder of the landscape's beguilement,
all to take in the redwing's

riffle, a willowed spillway's
mantra of dementia, monkskull
mushroom's yellow glow amid deadfall

debris. No motion or edge is fallow
in the demesne of sinew, sawtooth
& the spooled worm of the brain, so I

get my hackles up high & whisper
words that may thread the maze of
my own ear's delicate songbones

as any season's ratchet gradually turns.
This is the ritual of search
& seizure in summer's buzz & gnat

frenzy, or the artillery of breakage
in a winter wood, all racket
& understanding possible

as I am one, unredundant, so naive
every release seems complete manumission,
so dazed every feathering seems

a wing, & again, this is not to
testify to my terminal simplicity, but
I want to get it all wound tight

as an owl's pellet in the dewy grass
or a dung beetle's bundle, & the rustic
mask is what I add to blind luck to court even

the most elusive, cosmopolitan muse,
for I emanate faith as the glib
spider emits a silk to travel on

through the transluminous morning when
stargrass & wet snagweeds glisten
their iodine gold. Enchanting are

the drainsap's amber, even
sleet-glare and ants, as well
as the most civilized tear & articulate

laughter basking with cherry larks
in imagination's precincts
where the bedlam of briars gives way

to a nest, a firepit before
the lean-to lodge or some
other site with kindred mien whose

purpose & nuance
is tribal &
perfectly clear.

2.

LIFE LIST

Blear-eyed and solitary,
I study the lake at dawn.
Binoculars and a black
notebook keep me company
in this dry blind, but
nothing stirs marsh reeds
or disturbs the gray air.
My tenth winter of willing
indenture to this listing,
I scan the ragged treeline
and recall magpies pecking
litter from ash, a maverick
bunting fencing with his
image in a garden mirror or
the osprey's nest with its
cracked bough ready for
collapse. So many entries,
vigils, pretenses—I become
fir or a barkless snag,
an odd rock under goshawk
circles—anything to help
me blend in and eavesdrop,
any camouflage for my sly
voyeur's form. From habit
and instinct I follow my
field guide's advice on
habitat and music to catch
another bird's name, to
cage him in lined paper,
add a date beside cactus
wren, swamp sparrow, Bell's
vireo with a red berry,
a wet gnatcatcher perched
on the bent willow limb.
Once a fishing spoonbill
spread roseate wings like
Victory, and I mis-stepped
and fell into a ditch. Once
a mockingbird pecked my head.
Wood duck, Sabine gull on
driftwood, a male kittiwake
soaring or the anhinga with
a meter wingspan—all have
appeared beside thin birches
bright as birdsong or under

opalescent clouds. Each bird
gave evidence of such zest
and the pleasure of flight
I am drawn back to forest
and water for more sustenance.
Crouching now, I can taste
bacon grease and yearning
while a ruddy duck approaches,
then follows another cove,
awakening my old envy of all
grace and dazzle these beasts
harbor in their hollow bones,
lightness of mantle and scapular,
instinct's swift rituals,
and I am drifting myself, half
dreaming when the duck darts
to bare timbers shivering
in mist. Then his soft wings
oar the air, and I raise
the Zeiss to catch in round
lenses the low dip and levitation,
the sudden star of his wild
and transforming eye.

FIRE BLIGHT

Mid-Lent. An agate
sky. The March stars
are gone, the yard

still penitential,
though already the silver
maple whose symmetry

offered winter
comfort displays its
new leaves, and already

they wither inward
with the fire
blight. Who knows

how it comes—
airborne, bird-carried
or just coded

in the sapling's soft
marrows? The mystery
strikes like arthritis,

each leaf losing
all articulation
and sheen, then

shrinking to ash,
invisible flames licking
their way heartward,

and though this dying
is not loss of love
nor even its absence,

I am further shaken
by the ribwork fence
listing and yesterday's

crippled house finch
at the window box,
as if all natural

collapse corresponds
with some burning inside
me. The jittery wind

rattles dry branches,
and though I would
love to trim and spray

the doomed maple,
nurse it like a child,
I know blight will

have its way, scorching
the green, till
cell by cell, it is

ruined, left skeletal
to bewilder the songbirds
who sought its shelter,

as well as this one
witness, penitent by
the window and wondering

if the keener lesson
lies in the bud's
frail gesture toward

resurrection, or
in the way spirit
gives in to sorrow,

the ardent will failing,
the best intentions
gone slowly to smoke.

WALTER ANDERSON'S J

For his alphabet the painter
chose this blue quarreler
and lifted him out of nature

to perch eternal over pine
and cypress, his Prussian
feathers, jet crest and fine

profiled eye angel-elegant
in the sabal palm. The print
above my hearth is irreverent

and wild. The turned bird's
beak points to the russet word
of his name, floating absurdly

in swamp foliage silkscreened
on rice paper. His sin
amid the tree's scalloped fans

is pride, framed behind glass
that holds the winter of my face
as well. His gulf-coast curse

is almost audible on nights
when Jeremiah's just flights
of bitter rhetoric ignite

me and every letter shivers
like wind in a jay's feathers.
The painter rendered him vulgar

as he is in nature, sibylline
and raucous, a washed heaven's
pure verb silent in art's prison,

ravenous, indigenous and kin.

BIRDS, IN THE VIGOR OF MEMORY

In the twilight moonrise, the living
birds resist their eviction
with a frenzy of wings
and voices. The frail
light lifts them, as I remember the fallen:

daft mockingbird undone by
the kitchen window, chickadees that fell
frozen by the well,
a jay the smoky cat finally
caught and stripped down
to twigs and entrails. Under

the ruined garden, even one
pine siskin rusts amid the peavines,
and I consider the vigilant
appetites rasping, then
their icy vowels as they failed,
feathers giving up,
the light skulls, spoil

of muscle and fluted bones
gone to chalk. So many
measures of flight
and aria are always dissolving
to debris, and the living
respond in evensong
delirium. It's as if the fallen

could wrest sap and fresh strength
from this lamentation, could
regather from ghosthood their sleekness
and the oils of flight. Revived,
they might lead me or anyone attentive

to the sweet backrush of evening
toward some new star or a brightness
any pilgrim would follow
even the dead to. Again
and again toward the shining measure

of ripeness, the darkness gathers
as birds fly,
incandescent, almost delivered
from gravity's claw and
remembrance of nightfallen dew.

HAFT BLOSSOM

Eased by sunlight and trough
water from dream's secrets,
I found the axe after dawn
anchored in the oak stump,
vines wilder than morning
glory twining the ironwood
helve's curve, and high
on the arch where sap slowed
and the grain pooled most
stubbornly, a blossom of no
name arose, its petals bronze
in dewflash. Between my dry
garden and a cut cord of ash
and hickory, a marvelous
flower where my left palm's
sweat had altered wood was
sending forth shoots of light,
fragrance, blessing against
shadows, as if the voices
of angels riding sunshafts
had touched haftwood amid
the still, birdless forest
to say, "This is the center;
let there be no more dying."
As I grasped the handle
and pulled skyward, I saw
the red blade dangling roots,
felt the green vines snapping,
heard the passage of song
as the blossom dissolved
under my witnessing hands.

ALTER ALL

Here in the kitchen clean
as a cat's mouth,
I watch the light crawl
across blue tiles
and climb the blond wood
of table, cabinet
and counter. The blinds
slant daylight's
old desire to trespass and
transform the spices,
wine bottles, the fixtures
of bright chrome.
The bud vase from Venice
sits green as
a cat's eye transfixed by
calm woodgrain
and bends rays with its
column of water.
Light ascends to pale stem
and sepal, is if
they resembled a chancel,
or the mind, then
seizes the single lily's
petals, so yellow
they seem to lick the dust
from every corner.
The whole room glows, Italian
and Renaissance,
a chamber in della Francesca,
warm to the touch,
though mice snug as monks
plot in the cupboard
and a patient fly inscribes
his blasphemy in
dazzling air. He is certain
carrion is nearby,
sure the lily will wilt in
spite of my vigil.
He, also, knows sunlight's spill
must alter all
luster toward penumbra, slow
penance, the blessed
eloquence of decline.

WATERCOLORIST

On days when rain drums
the site trailer to say,
No work in this, you perch
in a motel room with coffee
and CNN to clean your
bouquet of brushes and mix
colors in a muffin tin.
Building codes and gripes
from contractors aside,
you hover over the deckled
paper, as if to capture
a sweetflag stem exactly
or register every iota
of thistle were a moral
issue. The simple wash
of willowy backdrop done,
you suffer for the details
and balance the sapless
tint of a small stalk
against civil wars, African
famine and your own exile
to rural Georgia where
another Wal-Mart or strip
mall lies implicit in blueprint.
The downpour hazes red
stripes of surveyor's tape
and umbers a bulldozed
acre. Charcoal of a larch's
wintering trunk, dirty
pearl of mistletoe berry,
staghorn sumac's cabernet—
you labor into the night
to hold winter's ache closer
as the TV rehearses its
quick increments of sorrow.
Slow stroke, crosshatch, blot
and scumble—one sure facet
of the outside world holds
credible and still inside
the Travel Inn's dingy
room, and the rain reminds
you to work quick and wet,
rill and feather the colors,
keep a steady hand and get
it right to stay alive.

DRIFT

Some nights the monster insomnia
could not be calmed in the bed
of polished mahogany or the hammock

strung between the strong post
oak and the one lightning jagged,
so he would bathe in insecticide

and make his way downhill, two
oars and a sack of canned Coors
slung over his shoulder. Through

sharp sawgrass and rushes on a path
glittering with malachite even
under sparse stars, he would walk

half awake to the pier where a rope
held the lapped boat ready. Water,
he thought, was a sure remedy for

whatever kept his mind from dream.
He read there was hunger everywhere
and war more places than peace.

Night was his time for concern
that the crippled governor was evil,
that his nation lacked worldly grace,

and he could not escape unless
he eased over the gunwales and slowly
rowed to the center, there to anchor

and lie back, letting beer dull him
and the lulling pond in a mild wind
shape an unseen pattern around him.

Then as crickets resumed chipping
their sparks of voice against the dark,
he would feel the beast's breath lift.

He would fall centuries back to
the thrift of sleep, a white center
in the mind as relaxing as ice

on the tongue in summer. He never
spoke his lake dreams to friends
but once slipped a hint that he woke

to dawn fog as fine as a shredded
afterbirth, then light and one white
bird rising in silence, a song

withheld, a curved feather left
to drift across a silver acre, toward
the anchor chain and morning.

SHRINE

Past the village
the stream meanders
and cuts stone slowly

with a saint's patience.
and in fact, on a bend
where the water skirts

a stand of willows,
the rocks open
into darkness, a grotto

where some peasant set
a statue of St. Ambrose,
and the farmers with

their women and afflicted
children have come for
decades to hang medals

and holy cards, to light
candles and say prayers to
the cave's deeper chambers

where the passage narrows
and no man has ever
been, but any witness

in summer can see
the quick dart of
workers and hear

the multitude buzzing
back in the shadows.
Some vow they can

smell the honey, that
water from the shallows
is sweeter by far.

Nearby flowers are
abundant, and the rumor
is that God or

some dark Madonna dwells in
the hive. In this
season of pollen drift,

bright wind in the cedars
and solace on the faces
of pilgrims, I also

listen for hymns in
the dark firs, suspend
all doubt and believe.

NACHTMUSIK

Listen. One by one
the wisteria
pods beyond the window

are popping
after three nights
of frost, and the beech

leaves, fallen
at last, curl,
each in its rind

of ice. A dog
scratches the storm
door. An oak log shifts

in the stove. Alone
here, I have learned
a little: how

the season whittles
back to bone,
how to stay warm

with no other
voice to sweeten
the room, how close is

anger, how cold.
As Orion strides
across the horizon

I imagine a host
of migrant birds
breathing easily

on the stripped
willow and along
telephone lines

stretching north.
Soft beads on
a rosary? Brown

flowers on a vine?
Never mind now. Sleepy
before the firescreen's

backlit fleur-de-lis,
I listen for seeds
spilling on the lawn,

rough-husked and patient
for April. In tune
with solitude's

calibrated tones,
sparrow by sparrow,
I count my way home.

3.

STAFFORD

It was in a diner.
He liked his coffee hot, but wasn't hungry.

Autumn, and across the highway
spider lilies and the frazzled
goldenrod blazed before the damp char
of a burned-out house.

He said poets are a natural phenomenon.
Metaphor is everywhere.
We are lucky if we learn,
he said, how to accept the gifts.

His face was weary
from writing, the weather
of steady thought. He spoke kindly,
but not of kindness, and gestured
beyond the distant treeline.

That's where we're going, he said.
The sumacs and yellow oaks
were already turning.
Mallards were on the wing.

I can still hear his voice in the herd
of deer seeking chestnuts
across the shining junkyard,
the color of a cardinal
blurring in the fire's green hymn.

Remembering thin smoke over the cup's rim
and the smell of scalded chicory,
I lift my eyes to the distant treeline
we are all slowly headed for,
and if I am not yet ready
for that resplendent gift,
then I am surely willing to be still
and hear the wilderness listen.

WALTER ANDERSON IN MISSISSIPPI

My God is a spiral
without beginning or end.
W.A.

Bird-mad and ruthless
in Shearwater Wood where the black skimmers
circle to become
song, the painter stalks
a swarm of monarchs or pauses
to quote his favorite psalm: *I will sing*
unto the Lord while I have my being.

Vermillion, bacchanalian
greens—all morning finches
and bitterns give him visions
in the *paille fine.* In his bullrush
nest he lies to sketch,
penning under the thistle-perched starling
on foolscap: *I do it, as always,*
in ecstasy.

Long-jawed and soft-spoken,
Anderson loves such halcyon days
that send him into tupelo
and paw-paw thicket humming *Te Deums*
or navigating his ramshackle
skiff by dead reckoning
across Biloxi Bay.

On Horn Island he sleeps
beneath his boat and keeps his camp
like a midden. By the driftwood fire
he sips red wine to remember
Selkirk's first delirium and Crusoe's
eventual calm, then dreams
of the day a cottonmouth caught
his arm in the sourwood copse
by Oyster Lagoon. All night
he fought a woodsfire
while the venom ran wild in his veins.
For two days he tossed in fugue.

Sweating at dawn, he recalls his escape
from the Whitfield asylum
on a rope of knotted bedsheets.
His bar of Ivory Soap
left the brick walls alive
with flying birds.

In his log, he scribbles at noon,
I will walk in sawgrass
and on water to draw unanticipated nature,
and thinks of his wife, patient

on the mainland, but a skunk, *poldeau*
or *becsie*—he savors the Cajun
names like manna—even the inevitable
pelican can drive him to paint
in frenzy, knowing soon
the poisons will burn this flyway
to garish waste and bones.

No repetition or symmetry
of image will still nature
or civilization's storm, yet he persists,
in spite of insect itch
and local ridicule, recording
thousands of forms. Overlap
of silhouette, a scumbled
wash and the fluent
line excite his passion
till heron and cooper's hawk levitate
above the page, agile
and radiant as church glass.

Protected by the swamp's moss
and windfalls, Anderson will ride out
Betsy alone and discover
in the hurricane's wake jewels moving
in sawgrass, till a scarlet
parrot steps forth, followed by a rainbow
of tropical birds
uncaged from Audubon Park
by the storm. In rapture,

he will paint them as fugitives and kin.

But today he settles
for a limber chain
of mallards circling the Strathmore
watermark. He pens
along the paper's weathered edge,
Birds are holes in heaven
through which a man may pass.

Above him, black flames
in the buzzard tree preen and threaten,
but he stops to feed
rice to a crippled heron
and watch sunset ember the horizon
trembling over his shoulder
as dark precedes him
shoalward, hearthward, home.

PAINTING OSCEOLA:
AN EPISTLE FROM GEORGE CATLIN TO HIS WIFE

Dear Kate,
First, my thanks for the lovely paperweight.
A dog of Mexican onyx is perfect to remind me
of what I set out to do. Missing you is more
than enough to make me abandon this mission,
and the summer miasma is nearly unbearable.
Already this morning I have walked long
under cottonmouth clouds that promise another
Charleston storm by afternoon. Hardly a soul
was about—a few carts delivering, Negro
women gibbering in Gulla as they arranged
bouquets for sale. I must say, in bondage
they seem to thrive. One great black hefting
a hogshead smiled at me with ivory and gold.
A tribe of children circled him like flies
as someone's trusted chattel swept Market Street's
enclosed stalls where field hands are sold.
But most whites still slept as I paced
down cobblestones brought over from Wales
and Scotland, ballast before the mast.
Of course, fragments of jagged cliff face
were soon replaced along the keel by chains
and the slaves they held to tame.

Among the town's festive petals, I, however, am free.
The loquats are ripe and fragrant, but the flavor
in them is not to my taste. No red wine can
mute it. And have I mentioned the dilemma
of oysters? Poisoned somehow by hard rains
that swelled the rivers and washed shipsealing
pitch out to the beds at sea. Add the fever
that sweeps the city's outskirts and you see
why I long to complete this portrait, and yet,
the dawn sky, crossed with rigging and flight
of slate and white gulls burns like a Turner
canvas, and I am inspired. I only hope
my subject will survive to the completion.

Yesterday I spent three hours with the chief.
Not in his cell. The dampness there is half
cause for his ailments. He is ready to die
and hardly listens to news and tales I bring.
I tried to tell him of Poe, who was stationed

under a traveling name in the same Fort Moultrie
that holds him in stone. The tales of treasure,
ghosts and sea oats shaping salt wind hold no
promise for a man dragged from his people, treachery
under the guise of treaty. When I walked today
past the hall, sporting its new cupola, where
Washington spoke of foreign folly, I felt shame
cut me to the heart. Certainly Osceola's
stabbing the old removal treaty with his knife
triggered a war that saw our boys die—darts
from blowguns and fever in the Florida swamp—
but who can blame the man who, I say over
and over, is no savage? Jackson determined
to send all the Seminoles west to desert
and hunger, or slay the entire tribe. The chief
described scenes of fired chickees, children
sliced in half by sabers. It is no wonder
he hates whites. No, I am no exception, but
he sees me as a sorcerer making evil he hopes
will damage those who look on his painted face.

Actually, Osceola is Creek, with the fine nose
of most Muscogean-speaking clans. The Spanish
named his branch *seminoli,* which means *wild*
or *runaway.* They have never trusted whites.
Darling, you should see him in his shirt
of ceremony, clay beads, turban with plumes
from egret, flamingo and bittern. Despite
what I take to be the sweats of cholera,
his eyes force the paints to find noble lines.
His every expression drives me to a finer
palette. My brushes are wild as marsh birds,
as if my hands were not the force behind.
In other circumstances, this warrior would
be revered as a god or prophet. What dignity!
I tell myself not to forget that he has
murdered, and Captain Dickinson always sends
a sentry with ready sidearm to protect me.
Don't fret. I'm safe as any man can be when
his own nation threatens savagery against one
as firm and true as this Osceola I paint now
even in my dreams, when they are not of you.

My coffee grows cold, and it is time to open
the Jamaican louvers that beckon seawind

and invite more light that I might face
my sketches, the charcoaled jaw and neck
corded with muscles that tremble. The bright
bay laurel outside rustles and skilled fingers
strum a soft guitar in a nearby garden.
Charleston serenades me to forget all.
This is far from the deprivation I usually embrace
when I let the gate to our front fence swing
and carry pigments and easel to mountain council
or winter camp. I dine on shrimp instead of
pemmican, listen to a spinet in the evening
or drink mint liqueur on the open gallery
when my mind is not on the art. The dog
you sent to keep my papers from scattering
brings to mind the iron leash that shackles
Osceola, who suffers also from arthritis
and is denied even a pipe, for the soldiers
know it is a power source for him. Love,
pray for the Lord to guide my hand, for
hurricane to hold off and for this land
that moistens with suffering and blood.
The man who eats hard bread in his cell
cannot, like me, turn a strong telescope
on its brass pivot affixed to the rail
and watch the clouds bank over the harbor's
stone forts. He feels no pride for
the flag that snaps in the breeze. I swear
he breathes at all only to curse his captors.
Today I cannot face his snarl as palmettoes
recall his native Everglades, the secret
trails, his wife's hands deft with beads,
graves of his sons in the swamp, the roar
of bull alligators in the mud. Kiss the boys
and promise them saltwater taffy and hammocks
on my return. I am anxious to see the sampler
you have been sewing and to taste wine
we said we'd save for a wonderful occasion.
If the Rousseau still troubles you, set it
aside and go back to Plato for more comfort.
Now I must return to today's problem: his
haunted eyes. I will bring you violet
shells, wicker baskets, my own flawed self
and some surprise. Your adoring husband,
George.

AUDUBON'S CARDINAL

The ailing artist shivers
in Vieux Carré and pulls
his Seminole jacket tighter,
then leans across to catch
an imagined flicker of eye.
The bird rendered on paper
stiffens, but he tells
himself it's not guilt
that prevents the miracle.
Heron, bittern, junco and
vulture—he's killed them
by the hundreds, but always
with one ambition, to sketch
a song in two dimensions—
insinuation's color and line.
Audubon lifts the cup
of chicory to his lips,
then turns again. He wants
the cardinal alive, a stalled
forager perched curious
on a mulberry limb in autumn,
but the eye, despite his vigor
and precision, shines like
glass, the red wing brittle
as ice. His most expensive
brushes, pigments shipped
from Paris, his practiced
articulate eye—they miss
the blasphemy he's after.
He almost laughs to recall
the day he perched high
on a sweetgum limb to watch
a brace feeding, the female
quick and oblivious over
a scatter of seeds, her mate's
brassy *chak,* the pitch
of a musket's dry cocking.
Hours he has labored. Now
primaries litter the table.
Small blades. A convex lens
any taxidermist would envy.
The original skull yellows
on the sill, and Audubon

coughs, rises to wipe bristles
and bloody spittle on a rag,
then turns to his journal
and scratches with a goose
quill in sinuous cursive
graceful, almost, as flight:
cul de sac, this work is
madness, yet I'll try again.
Sleet spatters the pane,
as he lifts his silver
flute from a Persian shawl,
and scarlet music flows
as through a living bone,
improvisations against rigor,
cardinal cantatas till dawn.

GOYATHLAY

Athabascan for "yawner," a boy's
habit before he learned the secret
language of the raiders, before
the elders knew he was a far seer.
He ran after the jackrabbit
and killed sidewinders with stones.
He prayed in the hogan or rode
his father's horse to bring
more corn to the tiswin makers.
He shot his arrows at rain crows.
On the mesa he spoke to storm clouds,
and the women loved him. His voice
was hard as chert. It was darker.
A Chiricahua, he followed Cochise
across the border and earned
fame for stealing. The Mexicans
who had coined "Apache" from Zuñi
words for "enemy," called him
"Geronimo." "Jerome," a saint's
name that intrigued him. A war
leader, stoic, often wounded, he
saw the new reservations abolished
and took to the mountains,
drinking rain, gnawing on belt
leather. We know the story:
he was invisible, a nightmare,
a treacherous demon with genius
for guerilla moves, the perfect
desert creature, a Gila monster
adored by his warriors: Naiche,
Perico, Mangus and Fun. Chatto
he thought was the brown servant
of Chi-den, the Great Evil. He
strove to honor Ussen, the Greater
Good Spirit. He spoke Spanish.
He shot cattle and rose from sage,
from caliche and mist, from nowhere,
a myth with a Winchester, a wraith,
an icon of absolute scorn.
Hummingbirds on the ridge swarmed
to the flash of his red bandanna.
Untrackable, he eluded even Tom
Horn and painted his face purple

with the yellow sunstripe. Then
he surrendered, calling it wisdom,
calling it medicine and fatigue.
After the Skeleton Canyon Treaty
he was sent east on the Southern
Pacific. In San Antone the crowd
wished to lynch him. He sold his
buttons for souvenirs. By candles
he sewed on more. At Fort Pickens
he and his kin suffered from miasma,
the Florida climate. He smoked
cigars and stared at tourists.
A debutante fainted. He learned to
weave baskets, to till the soil.
He advised his children and wives
to obey their captors in silence.
He rarely slept and stared at stars.
He scrawled autographs and met
the young Walter Reed. He spoke
to the ocean and walked alone,
homesick for the White Mountains.
More magician than council chief,
he remembered General Miles as
a man with a sneer. His torso
was strange with scars, an eye cut,
half shut forever. Lead lodged
in his tendons. He limped. In '94
they shipped him out west again,
to Fort Sill, after his wife Ga-ah
died of Bright's. He played cards
and wore an officer's blue tunic
over his long shirt. For a quarter
he would print his name on bows
he carved. He loved tortillas
and would not eat hog. He taught
the prisoners to boil the salt
from their water. Always he was
a chanter, though his son Chappo
was the best dancer. In Oklahoma
he joined the Dutch Reformed and
took another wife. He gambled
and saw Christ as divine. Goyathlay
still saw the wide spirit world
but could no longer cure the Ghost
Sickness. In Roosevelt's first

inaugural gala, he waved at
his old enemies. In Saint Louis
he was a World's Fair attraction,
a man who had murdered and run
wild in the shadows, a bewildering
eater of cactus and roots. He
watched the sunrise to recall
the *heshke,* the killer craze,
with sadness and ached for *piñon*
and ocotillo shade. He worked
in the garden and wove the willow.
His family and clan loved him. He
drove to market and made the laws.
At eighty, still pious, still fierce,
he fell from a wagon, drunk on
his craft sales. He died alone,
an exile who yearned for canyons
and rock sheer, spoor and a circle
of elders, magpies rising against
red dawn. He could hear dust
blowing and ponies at great distance.
He gave his name to our acts
of airborne abandon. He mourned
the wilderness as it vanished.
He wept only in his cold cell.
He killed with no venom and kept
vigils. Named for a saint, he swept
away with the wind but visits us
still. He yawned and chased arrows,
a boy who ran with the antelope,
a man who hid behind the moon,
who almost saved a renegade nation,
a man who fasted in the rain.

A BRADY PHOTOGRAPH OF LEE

Late in life, between Appomattox
and the college, the general stands
still for Brady's black box
and powder pan. Braidless,
white hat in hand, a sinner
unpardoned by Congress,
he poses before a closed door
in inverted image, not quite
in focus, three tarnished stars
burning his lapel, but dimly.
He can sleep well only on a cot
and harbors no hope of amnesty.

Then the nearsighted photographer
rushes into the Union hearse
he still uses for a darkroom.
Dashing the plates in fixer
and easing the features out,
he concentrates on the face,
his hands stinging in the mixture
until the unsmiling eyes assert,
two quiet rifle barrels waiting.
Extracting the print, Brady squints
as if to follow the process,
and Lee's features slowly clarify,
at last, the private cost, four
years of ghostly smolder
and the final, personal burning.

CROCKETT IN THE MOUNTAINS

Kettle Creek, East Tennessee, the Blue
Ridge fading. He rummages his possibles
while a brace of sweet quail sizzles
on willow spits that sprung the snare.
The fire's snap recalls his father's
Ulster brogue. He props against
the fruit-heavy ash and scrawls in his
log: *Fox in the Laurel slick, Gentian*
and Thistle abundant, good camp soft
in the last Orchids, the Maples are
flaming. After He sent them Quail
in the Wilderness, He sent Manna, but
glad this is not Marah, where Waters
were too bitter. I do miss Elizabeth,
and I miss whiskey. He can hear his
Congress watch ticking in his pocket.
He thinks of Polly, his year as
a widower, bondage to morning milking,
collecting eggs or following a plow
down doomed rows, rag "scholar" mocking
from his crossed sticks. He can still
swing an axe or wring a pullet's
neck, but would rather burn windfalls
and wade through goldenrod, Killdevil
at the ready and rusty eyes filled
with cardinal crest, sumac, dock
and deer scut. His hackles still rise
over absence and domestic unsuccess—
well dry, ticks everywhere, the meal
bin empty and his wife's unanswered
prayers. And what of the famous
Crockett wit? He shot the sacred cows
in the Capital and knew the feel
of velvet and brandy, but was not
Jackson's homespun lackey and refused
to uproot the Creeks. Every night,
even in elegant hotel suites, he
checked his powder and locked flint,
as he does now. Wens on his cheek,
arthritic fingers withering: is it
a judgement? He wonders, writes: *Few*
Critters and too much Excess latched
to my Name, though I can still snort

and curse with the Savagest, but am not
Nimrod Wildfire. Time to absquatulate
and have a look around. Still awed
by birch, the chapel of blue spruce,
he holds his breath, runs a butcher
blade across the whetstone and hears
a chinkapin's fall. Over hemlock
and oak, Orion strides, but he has
never learned to name all the stars
past Bear, Dipper, Hunter. Redsticks
could walk on leaffall and never
make a sound, but he could match their
mysteries. Mosquito burr, an owl
now black in the black elm. Finished
with the birds, he licks his fingers
and wonders if Boone found elbow
room where he went, if the waters
there were bitter. He takes a long
drink from his gourd. His new brood
will need space. A man needs time
and inspiration. He douses the fire,
listens to hiss of creekwater across
the embers, his father's Irish advice:
when all fruits fail, welcome the haw.
Why remember now? Already he's drowsy,
curious with sundowning thoughts
that catch him each evening: what
is left? He's fifty, his destiny
behind him. This is the whittling
that time does to manwood, slivering
the bark, blonde lumber and sapwood,
afterwards, the heart, and what does it
matter? Fame and friends can't halt
the sense of waste. To end the day
he enters: *Foxfire on the mossed*
Floor to the southwest and my own
restless Voice call me—"This way
to Cottonwoods and Prickly Pear
beyond the Mississippi Shore." We
make our own Manna, sweeten our
desperate Waters. Orion down, now
the Owl's Hour. Fire gone to Embers.
Sleep comes easy. He shifts his
feet and hears the predator's tremolo,
then far wingbeat; he is drifting

into a sleep sweet as early winter,
fog above a slow river, white night
and angels climbing a ladder toward
fire, toward his wanderer's wish
for a sign. Not hearing the owl's
call as warning or hymn, Crockett
falls deep in the thicket of longing's
loss. Displaced, wry and wasting
away, he is dreaming blood on his
palms and starved for New Eden, after
allemande left and land speculation.
He is bound for a church in the Texas
where wind in the elms hums his name.

4.

THE NAMES OF TREES

Sycamore, birch, larch—I have
always loved the names of trees,
and they alone have kept me
from self-loathing. A boy
in the Smokies, I climbed the black
locust to see what the next cove
held blind beyond the ridge. Blue
spruce were sparkling. Later I
perched in my chinaberry cradle
and picked clusters of withered
fruit brown as the Cherokee
elders' faces. One day wandering
deeper in Owl Valley's woods,
I discovered—amid blackjack oak,
hackberry and silver poplar—an elm
scorched and hollowed, its bee maze
vacant in a crown chamber and
no bear sign showing. Standing
now by my staked crab apples not
likely to make it through winter,
I remember the thrill of entry,
a rank scent and showers of dark
pith. From within I could see
tupelo and buckthorn budding,
the creek willows dragging their
pale branches. I saw how the trees
sleep standing. They drop dead
hands that shrivel and go back
to roots as rations. They speak
the language of light. They are
starving angels that look over
us and divert lightning. I was
taken by the feel of woodpulp,
honey stains like sap. I felt
the bark jacket, volunteer shoots
stirring, bird hymn and silence.
No more twigs were branching,
a network of dry nerves. The last
roots were writhing. I stood,
a wick in that black candle.
I knew the stir of a blackbird
flock as they settled. I
was Saint Joseph of the Elm or

Ariel burning. Then the birds
floated their bones as one being,
a chorus singing *water elm, catclaw,
tamarack, ridge hickory.* My
shadow in that trunk clung
to my shoulders, and the tree's
history filled me, its sad shade
long across saplings, deer paths,
the red fox pausing. A horned
owl answered the moon. I tasted
mulch, woodmusk and the names
of trees—green, pale, bud-yellow,
rough and healing on the tongue.

GRANDFATHER'S HEARTH

A pair of black andirons
hammered flat to angels
and ice-edged with heat
spread their wings
as if to mask Pandemonium's
flames. What did it mean—
a shrine where sap crackled
and all timber dissolved
to infernal flowers
too elusive to name?
I stared at chaos for hours,
then carried the question
to bed beneath the rafters,
asking God if any sin
could so weight us
that we might burn forever.

The sills locked with rime
ice while northern stars
etched a colder scripture,
and just when it seemed
sleep would never deliver
me, the lamp was a quenched
cinder, the ceiling gone
to smoke, and I remember
dreaming the hearth's cache
altered to snowflakes,
the feathers in my mattress
light as ash, two seraphim
shriven and flown.

IN HARVEST SEASON

Deciduous as hardwoods,
the apple-pickers arrived in
rusty trucks to raise
their tents and lean-to's
in a meadow where sneezeweed
and wild carrot thrived.
Expendable but dangerous,
or so we were told, as we
played among crates and under
ladders. Father said to avoid
their children, urchins
taught early to steal, but
we knew better, wondering at
biscuit-brown skin and unkempt
hair, their rough and lovely
games. The older ones wore
tattoos and jewels we couldn't
understand, tobacco stains
on their fingertips, a kind
of secret, snarling smile.
High amid bending boughs they
chattered in a traveling
slang we heard as music till
Father, archaic on horseback,
shoo-ed us, and soon all
the stems were twisted free
and ripening fruit waited
for the train. The final night
they drank jars of hard cider
and gambled their pay. After
a bedside story and mother's
tuck-in kiss, we crept out
the window to marvel
behind the laurels over
mandolin tunes, laughter
and anger flashing. Rag-tag
children danced in circles
to the snap of burning
applewood, their faces

stained with ash. Flames
climbed the night, leaves
ready to migrate and die.
Next day in the trampled
field, amid garbage middens
and dew, we stirred the smolder
with a twisted limb, chased
through the orchard against
Father's orders. We called out
to each other in a traveling
cant and sang of bonfires.
We devoured windfalls beside
the open road and marked our
scrubbed faces with char.

APPLE VOYAGE

Meadow grass green in harvest season,
its Sargasso rolled in raw autumn
wind. Cowbacks arched like dolphins.
A child in an apple tree could not
be Columbus's sly cabin boy, but
I perched in the spartan's high fork
to watch field hands I called *Indians*
as they cut the browning stalks
and shocked them like huts. What
was I after? Eleven, I was intent
on the western treeline no queen
had asked me to explore. No captain
with an astrolabe had sent me aloft,
but I had to scramble up past
bees from the hollow bough's socket,
bark scraping my bare chest,
every limb potentially brittle
in my hand. This was discovery.
This was risk. Desperate
for dream, I ascended. My crow's nest
smelled of amber sap; the limbs
were bound with rags to prevent
plentiful fruit from cracking them.
"That boy," grandmother said, "can't
keep his head out of the clouds.
He don't know pie dough from hen shit.
He's got no temperament for chores."
I hid among the dying leaves and kept
a log in my mind: *morale down,
monsters off our bows, we dispatched
two with our lombard, the pitch
of sap I smell is not the* Pinta's
*seasoned timbers but the forests
of Asia calling.* Thistle floss
and woodsmoke sailed with me over
a crew of chickens and stakes stacked
for spare rigging. I had to enact
some voyage, to follow leaves
as they changed toward first frost
and the future. Amid red fruit

I rode that caravel's mast
toward a new world and the sunset's
ripe color. The true course I set
followed the apple heart's bitter
star of seeds into evening chill
black as a Bible. At supper
I claimed a day of killing barn rats,
then wished for homework, prayer
and sleep. I updated the log: *taut*
hawsers and aching cables, yet
the deck is level, the sea flat,
calm as an apple's core, and still,
mystery of mysteries for us all
to behold, we seek east in west,
follow our star and navigate by dead
reckoning under the Spanish sail.

GHOST DANCE

A century too late, we stripped off
our khaki and badges to become
Wavoka's followers for the Boy Scout
Circus, though twelve boys could not
have saved one Sioux warrior
by believing that elkskin shirts
could turn back bullets. Craft
booths closed, the lashing exhibit
stopped in knots and chariot
race done, the lights went down
as dim drumbeats surrounded
the crowd. Spotlights caught us.
We dropped our robes and shone—
feathers, breechclouts, our limbs
dusted in flour. Six months we had
listened to the Paiute messiah's
stories every Wednesday night
and practiced dancing between
the Pledge and the Laws, so when
smoke rose white in our circle
and snowlight seemed to touch us,
we moved to the sacred cadence.
Carrying lances, the tortoise
rattles and antlers of enchantment,
we did the hop step, the eagle
crouch and fancy dancer's sweep,
as if Custer and Sitting Bull
were newly dead and a slow-motion
circle of children enacting the last
catastrophe could step through
dreams to see the world begin over,
could unearth whole bones till
the buffalo once more cast their
shadows on the Great Plains. It was
a wild west show to rival Cody's
on the verge of fresh adolescence.
It was a trance of understanding,
but it passed in sweat, gooseflesh,
the salt-sting of shielded tears.
Now the passing seasons—Moon
of the Chokecherries, Moon of Sweet
Grass, Wolf Moon—raid the past.
To summon it back I take whiskey
in the kitchen, crouch in the shape
of a ghost and brace my floured
limbs for the absence of drums,
salt, the familiar shock of loss.

WATER MOTH

Not possible, of course, but what if
the wingdust's agate patterns
would not dissolve in salt water
and the bones finer than needles
would not fail? Recalling Father's
blue morphos, the poseidons, matched
sulfurs, violets and swallowtails
all still in their cases, I long for
a winged rorschach quick as a nymph,
a noctuid in silver that no one
could collect and smother, nobody's
nemesis. No hobbyist's monograph
on their habits or breeding case
could exist. The water moth would
breathe where no air is, and its
caterpillar must be a bottomfeeder.
I imagine the still chrysalis
thriving undersea, clinging to coral
or driftwood as a whelk in soporific
depth, till the newborn moth gnaws
free to feed on algae. So many
slight manta rays, almost, they would
swoop and soar in the Gulf Stream
or mate in Pacific currents, too
small for any net, their eyes honed
to the dark and thin scales strong
as a carp's. No purpose, of course,
but to elude the collector's
bottle and shadow box, to gather
in multitudes for migrations when
deep brine chills. I want them safe
from chaffinch and missel thrush,
harmless as sea horses, the stuff
of legends mad for some unknown sap
in the sea's breath, their azure,
jade and chicory wings never to be
touched by forceps, not one specimen
ever pinned through the thorax,
glassed in and framed with mankind's
notions, his numbing Latin names.

CHICKADEES

Where do they come from, turning up
after cold has killed the insects
and the tanager and redstart have gone?

All summer they threaded the tangle
of thicket or domestic hedge, shadows
tending to nest and young, modest

beside the oriole's flash or robin's
perfect song. But now the leaves
are down and frost ferns the pane.

Morning finds one coal starring
the darkened hearth, a chill swelling
in every room and a tribe of chickadees

hopping on brown grass, seed-desperate
but dependable as starlight or wind,
delicate, but likely to last the winter.

And why do I stand beside the window
in sight of my unfinished woodshed,
content to sip sweet almond tea

and wonder at the caretaker birds
husbanding slim pickings, tediously
policing every inch of brittle lawn?

One works at a weed's unspent seed
cluster for an hour's better part.
Another digs at the shadow side

of a rotting log, but the mass perform
a dance of vigilance, the habit
of persistence framed by quick flight

and indelible song. Soon the first
flakes will collect in clouds to fall:
winter, blizzard, solitude. All

the last rations will be concealed
and nothing will feed the chickadees,
unless I scatter seed to nourish

them as they, briefly, now nourish me.

THE USES OF ENCHANTMENT

Thinking of sorcery, I imagine Merlin
as the oak yearning to speak. Locked
between bark and heartwood, spellbound
by the ravishing apprentice, he must have
felt some regret over the lore he
gave her, the passion and craft. It was
love that struck him blind. How
he could not fail to see that Vivian wore
snakes as bracelets, the dragon's amulet
in her eyes. How he opened his Druid
heart. How she pantomimed pleasure
and lied for his secrets. What was
the riddle she asked? I have to wonder
why his answer doomed him to trance.
I imagine the wizard immobile, a bare
tree with ravens. How they roosted
in his branches and limed his trunk,
their cold voices withering his roots
like winter. How his tongue strained
toward words to lament youth's devoted
cruelty, yet how every syllable he
gave the wind still praised her beauty,
how closely his pain resembled joy,
though the tree, if it could speak,
would surely testify, *pain is never joy.*

LEGACY

In roadside litter the *S*
of a snake stripped
and nibbled to a million ribs
lies clean as wicker
and white as magnolia sheen.
Gone are jeweled skin,
the split tongue that flickered,
the quickest transit
in swamp water or
marsh grass. The only
vital signs are borrowed,
red scavengers where once
the spine shot its edict:
strike, and strike again.

Even the fire ants scatter
at a handful
of thrown grit,
and in the small skull
two fangs still glitter,
catch sunlight far
from the garden, apples,
any forbidding angel's flame.

An indecent image, I admit,
the tempter's symbol—
yet I would touch it,
feel the artifact,
shorn and exquisite,
twisted as the initial
of my inherited name,
the false sin of invention,
the myth of shame.

5.

PLAYING THE BONES

Two sticks curved like ribs,
the new moon—I grip them
between proper fingers
like a heron's talon around
a fish. Still, I listen
to the sea in Sean Nations'
fiddle, surf curling cool
from Mick Tracey's flute.
When the need for a sleek
bird skirting shore fills
me, I find the quick pendulum
in my wrist and give
to music the clack and rattle
of a great blue's hinged
beak. I settle sweetly
into the rhythm, discrete,
one right thing syncopated
with the pearl sky low over
Galway Bay. While the mist
of a tin whistle rises
to show us a way back
to silence, I pantomime
something; say, a farewell
wave or wingbeats over gray
water; say, some hunger
for simple invention, a path
through whin and the wind's
whisper. I seek a passage
to melodic breath, a nest
in the waterweeds, solace
after the barman locks up
and I wind these bones warm
in their flannel cloth
and under a hint of moon
walk myself home to sleep
and the dream of hollow
birdbones, stitch by stitch
knitting a soothing tune.

KILCOOLIE FERN

Friday night's ritual fish,
a whole rosary and votive
candles all cache in this

skeletal ditch-bank fern
beside ruined Kilcoolie
Abbey. Even the broken

stones remind me of kitchen
devotions amid the reek
of grease and Gillette

Razors' TV boxing match.
Plaice, flounder and red
salmon were all I understood

of the Catholic madness,
the penitence and fasting,
yet this abandoned site

reels me in with its vetch,
dandelion and sheep dip,
a glittery birdcall high

in the summer air. Is it
twilight etching every leafy
thing to mystery that lures

me, or the mermaid carved
like a fossil beside
the chancel arch to say,

There are two worlds? When
I touch her for luck, she
becomes at once Blue Mary

and my mother. Her chiseled
fish are children swimming
to be fed. Dusk now. Azure

mist. St. Patrick's crazed
angel in granite overhead
becomes Gillette's mascot macaw

squawking on the screen, my
father the heretic tossing
raw curses at the Pope,

and I am again the child
divided between two sects.
Beer charges the sitting room

air. Anger follows, a slap,
and I am hiding under a plaid
duvet. Who in this abbey's

wreck plays the Protestant
cleric ringing at our door,
if not the chipped face

of Thomas Martyr carved low
on a secular bier? Blackfaced
merinos graze in silence

as the Celtic mermaid fades
with first dark into gray
stone, her thin ribs gone

so faint I'm not sure I
ever saw them, the fern's
spine now at the Angelus

hour offering a green
ladder I would ascend
to base my life on the hell

of hazel, ash bramble, wood-
bine and the orphan-spare,
memory-stirring lace

of fishbone fern.

SABBATH IN DONEGAL

In the amber of a March morning
one heron circles the sallow
dam, her sniper's eye slit
against the sharp light. Tea
on the hob steeps to the click

of knitting needles. Hooded
haycock, turfstack, a corner
bin rich with red potatoes.
A calf standing hock-deep
in the stream and sun simple

on the pump's handle complete
this picture of rural bliss,
but a riddled muffler scraping
the road interrupts. A black
Tom laps milk on the sill.

As wind quickens the locust,
the figure sitting almost
still at the window works
his soft cloth. The tune he
whistles under the Sacred

Heart is "Crock of Gold." Rush
cross, hurley medals, lace
on the table—who would guess
the shadow of an evening
secret fills this white house

with sorrow? The man's left
thumbnail is cracked to the quick.
Gray stubble shades his upper
lip. The dry snap of a mantle
clock echoes the ache of an empty

cradle in the kitchen. Against
the fox russet of this farmer's
jumper, the crow metal shine
of a Webley revolver rhymes hard
with the bishop's bell clanging

across wind-shaken Donegal Bay.

TINKERS

"He's not long off the road," the Irish
will offer as insult to anyone dark
and swarthy as he is surly. Bad
teeth, maybe heavy brows, callouses.
Once they were menders of tin kettles
and pans, sharpeners of scissors and
raspy knives. Their vans were bright
behind the horses they understood so
well their expertise was envied, if
only in passing. Now their cant is
a secret singing, their laughter full
of briars and beer, though today they
pitch their sad caravans at roadside
trash dumps the Dublin government
approves. The children beg and are
famous as thieves, but they harbor
a dark beauty no one else can breed.
The women weave the brightest colors.
Their suffering is well known, yet
caravan music can alter the air.
Rabbit catchers, comb robbers, shills?
"The Travelers," they style themselves,
and may camp or even build and settle
near Tuam, outcasts of a sort, but
one close look in a Tinker's liquid
eye, and you know a little something
of what was once their home. You see
compass and chart by lantern-glow, then
the famous storm. You hear splintering
masts and torn canvas, curses in
a darker tongue as the doomed Armada,
like the wandering tribes of Ireland,
seeks familiar stars, a friendly shore.

ON LARAINE'S GRAVE HILL

I walked from Kilronin and climbed
the wall, stepped over red clover
and a hare's pelt and skeleton
to find this site where Saint Enda
raised his first church. Centuries
later, it's a ruin amid the plots
of Monica de Burca, shipwrecked
Colm MacDonagh, and Mary Flaherty,
who never outgrew her cradle. I
could record the dates of a hundred
sleepers or lie down in this
drizzle forever to contemplate
man's passing, but I almost trip
into an open grave with its stone
already cut and set for Blind Sim
Mulkerren, dead this week from
a fall, who could no doubt have
taught me how to be bereft and
accept it. An angle-cut birch
slab is ready for his candle,
and as I consider the slow surrender
to worm, root and the earth's
warming weight, a shoal of birds
rises in the bay, their wingrush
saying, "The long sleep toward
heaven comes soon enough, you must
learn to live with loss," as
they vanish in mist. So I will
not join Michael Gill and his kin
under the primrose and maidenhair
fern, far from gull cries and raven's
ravenous bill. I will bid Enda's
hazardous chapel farewell, collect
a fist of cowslips for poor Mary
Flaherty and scrape my boots
on the sexton's spade to step over
the dead, half stumbling in dusk,
half dancing downhill, going home.

CHORE

Clockwork woke me
at the drover's hour. Stirred
embers and a slosh of tea.

The basket's handle
of woodbine twisted
as a linnet's song fit

my palm exactly. Dew
glittered the madder grass
and meadow chirr stilled

to my step. When the coop's
saddlehide hinge swung,
I stooped under the low

lintel, caught cobwebs
on my lips and crept
with otter stealth. No

russet-combed cock
stirred as purring hens
let me ease my hand amid

twilled straw and down.
With each egg nesting
in basket moss, a warm

moon kept its secret
dawn, though I walked
out under snowclouds

feathering the north
and sang my song
of plunder to a world

on the edge of freshness,
red ivy calmly dying
on the autumn wall.

MIST NET

As if some spider gone
scientific at twilight
has decided to snare

a herd of sparrows, I
raise my web between
hillside birches and

hope for a low moon
and scuttling in the brush
to startle the birds,

that I might hear
the wild wings thrashing
unharmed in nylon mesh,

that I might inspect
each hostage to verify
myths about size,

migration, the weight
of autumn feathers. All
science aside, I yearn

just once to caress
sleek necks, to feel
the fast hearts small

as burdock burrs against
my palm. I want to cast
them up, so many dark

stars soaring, wishbones
needling north above
the dry forest, briefly

blemished with my
human touch, secretly
burning with song.

A CATHOLIC EDUCATION

When Sioban said the nuns
warned against a high polish
on those pumps the convent girls
wore, I doubted her. I could
not imagine our Sister Mary
Immaculata claiming boys
would see white knickers
and have "the bad thought"
on the spot, but this morning
the TV news showed soldiers
with mirrors on hurley sticks
scanning beneath the chassis
of English Fords in Belfast. It was
car bombs they were after,
the neat gelignite cylinders or
a mercury fuse wrapped in pale
silk, and in my skeptical
objections to an Irish girl's
adolescent confessions I can
no longer feel wholly secure.

LITHOGRAPH

Mid-morning after a light frost,
and Liam in his studio is lifting
a wide sheet where the ink
silhouette of a sleeping deer
shines. Seeing him turn it

under the skylight, I imagine
the wounded doe lying down
in the dregs of darkness, the steam
of her life rising radiant
in the dawn. She is ready to begin

changing to dust and blossoms,
limbs dissolving to a dozen lines
nestled in limestone, as if the rock
were soft as windblown spindrift
under the craftsman's hands. This,

I am thinking, is the way nature
makes a fossil—muzzle, white rib
and long bones folding, mossed over,
the edges giving way to texture,
a thousand years of afterthought

holding to what must not disappear,
but Liam's hands have caught
the process, fine lines embedded
where the press will kiss them,
and it is not loss he presides over

but the possibility of vigor,
as the deer takes gracefully to this
dreaming, the eastern light raising
her in the artist's eyes, and the color
that could not be part of the dying

is still darkening his hands.

You might also enjoy these books from Livingston Press &
Swallow's Tale Press:

Poetry
Eugene Walter   *Lizard Fever*
ISBN 0-942979-18-4, paper $12.95
ISBN 0-942979-17-6, cloth $21.95

Michael J. Bugeja   *Flight from Valhalla*
ISBN 0-942979-12-5, paper $9.95
ISBN 0-942979-13-3, cloth $21.95

Charles Ghigna   *Speaking in Tongues*
ISBN 0-942979-20-6 $11.95

Stephen Corey   *Synchronized Swimming*
ISBN 0-942979-14-1 $9.95

Ralph Hammond, editor *Alabama Poets*
ISBN 0-942979-07-9, paper $12.95
ISBN 0-942979-06-0, cloth $19.95

Fiction
James E. Colquitt, editor   *Alabama Bound: Contemporary
Stories of a State* includes a story
by **R.T. Smith**
ISBN 0-942979-26-5, paper $13.95
ISBN 0-942979-25-7, cloth $24.95

Tom Abrams   *A Bad Piece of Luck* (novel)
ISBN 0-942979-23-0, paper $9.95
ISBN 0-942979-22-3, cloth $23.95

B.K. Smith   *Sideshows* (stories)
ISBN 0-942979-16-8, paper $12.95
ISBN 0-942979-15-X, cloth $23.95

Natalie L.M. Petesch *Wild with All Regret* (stories)
ISBN 0-930501-07-1 (Swallow's Tale) $10.95

R. T. Smith works at Washington and Lee University as editor of *Shenandoah.* His books of poems include *The Cardinal Heart* and *Trespasser,* and his book of stories is *Faith.* His work has appeared in *Poetry, Poetry Ireland Review, Gettysburg Review,* and *The Irish University Review.* He has received fellowships from the NEA and Arts International. For twelve years Mr. Smith was Alumni Writer-in-residence at Auburn University, and in 1994 he was a resident at Annaghmakerrig in County Monaghan, Ireland. *(Photo by W. Patrick Hinely.)*

Also Available from Livingston Press:

The Cardinal Heart, by R.T. Smith
ISBN 0-942979-09-5, paper $8.95
ISBN 0-942979-08-7, cloth $13.95

60 pages

"More than any book I've read in the past decade, this collection lifts my spirits and renews my faith in the value of poetry. . . .My joy at reading these poems derives from Smith's directness and honesty, his rejection of slickness on the one hand and self-indulgent confession on the other."
Don Johnson, in *Poet & Critic*
"R.T. Smith writes with a singular beauty of phrase and admits the heart's chaos without sacrificing accuracy, for his allegiance is to time and place, his references to nature and history."
Rodney Jones